Know Your
Bible
for Kids

Donna K. Maltese

Illustrated by David Miles

BARBOUR
PUBLISHING

Published by Barbour Publishing, Inc., P.O. Box 719, Uhrichsville, Ohio 44683
www.barbourbooks.com

Our mission is to publish and distribute inspirational products offering exceptional value and biblical encouragement to the masses.

ecpa Member of the
Evangelical Christian
Publishers Association

Printed in the United States of America.
Versa Press, Inc., East Peoria, IL 61611; November 2013; D10004208

Introduction

In 66 books, 1,189 chapters, and hundreds of thousands of words, the Bible shares one amazing message: God loves you.

From Genesis, where God creates human beings, to Revelation, where God dries all tears, the Bible proves that God cares very much about His people. His great love is seen in the death of His Son, Jesus Christ, on the cross. That sacrifice for sin allows anyone to be right with God through faith in Jesus.

These truths are found in the pages of God's Word. But sometimes they can be buried by the tons of information in the Bible. That's why *Know Your Bible for Kids* was written.

In this little book, you'll find short sketches of all 66 Bible books. Every entry follows this outline:

- *Who wrote the book?*
- *When was the book written?*
- *What's the book about?*
- *What's an important verse from the book?*
- *What does that mean?*
- *So, what?*

Use this book to begin a Bible journey—one that could change your life!

Genesis

Who wrote Genesis?

The book doesn't say—but most people believe it was Moses.

When was Genesis written?

Moses lived about 3,500 years ago—but the story of Genesis goes back to the very beginning of time!

What's Genesis about?

One word: Beginnings.

In more words: Genesis tells how God created the whole universe just by speaking. God spoke, and there was light and dark. God spoke, and the Earth had skies, seas, and land. God spoke, and there were plants, fish, birds, and animals. But then God made people specially—He created Adam from the dirt and Eve from a rib of Adam.

Genesis also tells us about
- the beginning of sin—when Adam and Eve disobeyed God in the Garden of Eden
- Noah and his ark full of animals
- a very important man named Abraham
- Abraham's kids, grandkids, and other family members—Isaac, Jacob, Joseph, and the "people of Israel"— God's chosen people

What's an important verse from Genesis?

And Abram believed the LORD, and the LORD counted him as righteous because of his faith. GENESIS 15:6 NLT

What does that mean?

"Faith" is believing in God—believing that there is a God, and that what He says is true. When we have faith in God, God is happy! (Learn more in Hebrews 11:6.)

So, what?

God made you for a special purpose—to walk close with Him. Your journey is just beginning.

Exodus

Who wrote Exodus?

The book doesn't say—but most people believe it was Moses.

When was Exodus written?

Moses helped God's people exit Egypt. He lived about 3,500 years ago.

What's Exodus about?

One word: Exit.

In more words: Exodus tells how God's people—the Israelites—became slaves in Egypt. When they cried out to God, He heard them. He raised up Moses to save them. After God sent ten plagues on Egypt, its king—or pharaoh—let the Israelites go. But then he changed his mind. So God parted the Red Sea and His people escaped.

Exodus also tells us about
- the Ten Commandments—God's list of dos and don'ts
- the worship of a golden calf
- God's pillar of cloud and pillar of fire
- manna—special bread from heaven

What's an important verse from Exodus?

"I have heard the groans of the Israelites. . . . Tell the people of Israel, 'I am the LORD. I will throw off the heavy load the Egyptians have put on your shoulders. I will set you free from being slaves to them. I will reach out my arm and save you with mighty acts." EXODUS 6:5–6

What does that mean?

When God hears our cries, He will help us—because He loves us. That's why He sent Moses—to save the Israelites. And that's why He sent Jesus—to save us.

So, what?

When you are in trouble, God will always help you find the exit.

Leviticus

Who wrote Leviticus?

The book doesn't say—but most people believe it was Moses.

When was Leviticus written?

About 3,500 years ago.

What's Leviticus about?

One word: Holiness.

In more words: Leviticus means "about the Levites"—people from the family of Levi. The Levites were to be the ministers for God. In Leviticus, God tells His people how to serve, obey, and worship Him—how to be holy. Then God lists all the blessings for obeying Him. It is a book full of rules—laws to live by.

Leviticus also tells us about
- what the people were to sacrifice
- which animals were okay to eat
- Moses' brother, Aaron, who was the first high priest
- special holy days like the Sabbath and the Passover

What's an important verse from Leviticus?

"Be holy, for I the Lord your God am holy."
LEVITICUS 19:2 NLV

What does that mean?

The word *holy* appears in Leviticus 150 times. It means to be pure and set apart—just for God and just like God. Back in Moses' day, people killed animals ("sacrifices") because God's people weren't holy. Later Jesus died on the cross to make us holy—one sacrifice, one time, for everyone.

So, what?

You don't have to follow the rules in Leviticus to be holy. But you still worship a holy God through Jesus Christ. So treat Him with respect.

Numbers

Who wrote Numbers?

The book doesn't say—but most people believe it was Moses.

When was Numbers written?

About 3,500 years ago.

What's Numbers about?

One word: Wandering.

In more words: Numbers starts by counting warriors—and that's how the book got its name. After counting 603,550 fighters, the Israelites begin a 200-mile walk to the Promised Land of Canaan. Because of the people's fear, naughtiness, and complaining, they wandered in the wilderness for 40 years! Numbers also tells us about

- spies reporting a land of giants
- the courage of Joshua and Caleb
- the earth swallowing up complainers
- Moses hitting (instead of talking to) a rock that God said would provide miracle water

What's an important verse from Numbers?

"If the LORD is pleased with us, he'll lead us into that land. It's a land that has plenty of milk and honey. He'll give it to us." NUMBERS 14:8

What does that mean?

Twelve spies checked out the Promised Land where giants lived. Ten spies said the Israelites were grasshoppers compared to the giants. Only two spies—Joshua and Caleb—knew that God is bigger than anything and anyone. They were faithful and brave. So God let only Joshua and Caleb into the Promised Land.

So, what?

Keep your eyes on God. He's bigger than any giant. And God won't let you wander. He will lead you to a land of plenty. That's a promise!

Deuteronomy

Who wrote Deuteronomy?

The book doesn't say, but most people believe it was Moses—except for the last eight verses. Those tell us about Moses' death.

When was Deuteronomy written?

About 3,500 years ago.

What's Deuteronomy about?

One word: Remembering.

In more words: In Deuteronomy, Moses is 120 years old. Forty years have passed in the wilderness. All the people who escaped Egypt are dead—except for Joshua, Caleb, and Moses. So Moses tells the Israelites the history of their wandering in the wilderness. And he repeats God's rules for the new generation. (The word *Deuteronomy* means "second law.")

Deuteronomy also tells us about

- Moses seeing the Promised Land from Mount Nebo
- Moses dying and being buried by God
- Joshua becoming the Israelites' new leader

What's an important verse from Deuteronomy?

"You saw how the Lord your God carried you, as a man carries his son, in all the way you have walked until you came to this place." DEUTERONOMY 1:31 NLV

What does that mean?

Moses reminded the people of the way God helped them. God did miracles for them—like parting the Red Sea so they could escape Egypt. He led them all through the wilderness. He provided special food called manna. And He carried them to safety.

So, what?

Never forget how God has blessed you. He carried you yesterday. He carries you today. And He will carry you tomorrow. You are safe in His arms.

Joshua

Who wrote Joshua?

The book doesn't say—but most people believe it was
Joshua, except for the last five verses. They tell about
Joshua's death.

When was Joshua written?

About 3,400 years ago.

What's Joshua about?

One word: Victory.

In more words: Moses has died. Joshua is the Israelites' new leader. And he is the one who leads them into the promised land of Canaan. God's words give the new leader courage. So Joshua leads his people into battle. The first stop—Jericho. With the help of God, the city walls fall down. The Israelites win the battle.

Joshua also tells us about
- Rahab and the spies
- God parting the Jordan River
- God making the sun stand still during a battle
- each tribe getting a piece of the Promised Land

What's an important verse from Joshua?

"Be strong and brave. Do not be terrified. Do not lose hope. I am the LORD your God. I will be with you everywhere you go." JOSHUA 1:9

What does that mean?

God told Joshua to be brave. He also told Joshua that He would be with him no matter where Joshua went. Joshua believed God's words. So he was able to lead his people to great victories.

So, what?

Do not be afraid of anything. You have God. He can do anything. And He is with you wherever you go. He will help you win any battle.

Judges

Who wrote Judges?

The book doesn't say—but some people believe it was the prophet Samuel.

When was Judges written?

About 3,000 years ago. But some of its stories take place as long as 3,400 years ago.

What's Judges about?

One word: Rescuers.

In more words: After Joshua dies, the Israelites take a break from chasing pagan people off their land. (Pagans are people who worship things called idols instead of God.) But God's people start worshipping idols, too. And that only gets them into trouble. When the Israelites cry out to God for help, He sends judges to rescue them.

Judges also tells us about

- Deborah, a prophet, wife, judge, and army leader
- Jael, a woman who killed a general
- Gideon and his fleece
- Samson and his great strength

What's an important verse from Judges?

In those days Israel didn't have a king. The people did anything they thought was right. JUDGES 21:25

What does that mean?

The Israelites were going in circles. First they'd disobey God. Then they'd cry out to Him. God would send judges to rescue the Israelites. And for a while they would behave. But then they'd go back to not obeying God— doing "anything they thought was right."

So, what?

The one and only way to stay out of trouble: Don't do what you think is right, but do what God says is right.

Ruth

Who wrote Ruth?

The book doesn't say—but some people believe it was the prophet Samuel.

When was Ruth written?

About 3,100 years ago.

What's Ruth about?

One word: Faithfulness.

In more words: Ruth was a woman from Moab. She married a Jewish man. When he died, she faithfully followed her mother-in-law—Naomi—to Bethlehem. Once there, Ruth needed work to keep them both fed. So she gathered grain in the fields of a rich man named Boaz, a relative of Naomi.

Ruth also tells us about

- Ruth leaving her home to live with strangers
- Boaz and Ruth falling in love, then getting married
- Boaz saving Ruth and Naomi from being poor
- Ruth giving birth to Obed—who became the grandfather of King David

What's an important verse from Ruth?

"I will go where you go. I will live where you live. Your people will be my people. And your God will be my God." RUTH 1:16 NLV

What does that mean?

When her husband died, Ruth could have stayed in her own country. That would have been the easy thing to do. But instead, she followed Naomi to a strange land. Because Ruth was faithful to Naomi, God gave her many blessings.

So, what?

When you are faithful to God, He will be sure to reward you. Trust in Him. Follow Him, and He will bless you.

1 Samuel

Who wrote 1 Samuel?

The book doesn't say—but some people believe Samuel may have written parts of it.

When was 1 Samuel written?

About 3,000 years ago.

One word: Kings.

In more words: Judges have been leading Israel. And God was the King over all. But now the people want a human king, like other nations. The priest Samuel doesn't think that's a good idea. But God tells him to make a man named Saul king. Saul makes many mistakes. So God tells Samuel to make David the next king.

1 Samuel also tells us about

- God answering Hannah's prayer for a son—Samuel
- the shepherd boy David killing the giant Goliath
- King Saul throwing a spear at David—two times!
- Jonathan and David's great friendship

What's an important verse from 1 Samuel?

The LORD told him, "Listen to everything the people are saying to you. You are not the one they have turned their backs on. I am the one they do not want as their king."
1 SAMUEL 8:7

What does that mean?

The Israelites wanted to be like other people—to have a human ruling over them. But when they took God off their throne, trouble followed.

So, what?

It's better to keep your eyes on God than people. Let Him—and no one else—be King of your heart and life.

2 Samuel

Who wrote 2 Samuel?

The book doesn't say. The author couldn't have been Samuel—he was dead when this book was written. Some people believe Abiathar, a priest, wrote it.

When was 2 Samuel written?

About 3,000 years ago.

What's 2 Samuel about?

One word: Kingdoms.

In more words: After King Saul is killed in battle, David becomes king of Judah. Later he rules all of Israel. He is a good warrior and wins many battles. But then David falls in love with a married woman, Bathsheba—and family troubles follow. His son Absalom dies trying to steal the kingdom. At the end, David rules all of Israel once again.

2 Samuel also tells us about

- King Saul and Jonathan being killed in battle
- David's greatest warriors—called "mighty men"
- a giant with six fingers on each hand and six toes on each foot!
- the birth of Solomon, the next king

What's an important verse from 2 Samuel?

"He saved me from my powerful enemies. He set me free from those who were too strong for me." 2 Samuel 22:18 nirv

What does that mean?

King David was a man after God's own heart—but he was also just a man. He made mistakes. And he paid for some of the bad things he did. But God was always there for David, ready to step in and save him again and again.

So, what?

You don't have to be perfect to serve God. Just be willing to love Him, know Him, and please Him. Let Him know you want to serve in His kingdom.

1 Kings

Who wrote 1 Kings?

The book doesn't say—but some people believe it was the prophet Jeremiah.

When was 1 Kings written?

These stories take place about 3,000 years ago. But the book was probably written about 260 years later.

What's 1 Kings about?

One word: Splitting.

In more words: After King David dies, his son Solomon becomes ruler. The new king begins to build a temple for God. Then the wise Solomon does something not so smart—he marries many foreign women who lead him away from God. When Solomon dies, the nation of Israel splits into two kingdoms—Judah and Israel.

1 Kings also tells us about

- King Solomon's throne of ivory
- the queen of Sheba's visit to Solomon
- the evil King Ahab and his wicked wife, Jezebel
- the prophet Elijah being fed by ravens

What's an important verse from 1 Kings?

"Because that is what you have asked for, I will give it to you. I will give you a wise and understanding heart."
1 KINGS 3:11–12

What does that mean?

When we pray, God will give us what we have asked for—if that's what He wants us to have. Solomon asked for wisdom—and got it! But then he began worshipping the gods of his wives. He turned away from the one true God. And his kingdom was torn apart.

So, what?

Don't let anyone split your heart from God's and His blessings.

2 Kings

Who wrote 2 Kings?

The book doesn't say—but some people believe it was the prophet Jeremiah.

When was 2 Kings written?

These stories take place from 2,800 to 2,500 years ago. But the book was probably written about 100 years later.

What's 2 Kings about?

One word: Going.

In more words: Going, going, gone! The kingdom is still split into two nations. Nineteen evil kings rule Israel. Then that nation is destroyed. Other kings—most of them bad—rule Judah, which is destroyed next. Almost all of God's people are taken away from their homes.

2 Kings also tells us about

- the prophet Elijah taken up in a chariot of fire
- God bringing a widow's dead son back to life
- the evil Jezebel falling out of a window
- God turning a shadow back ten steps

What's an important verse from 2 Kings?

Elisha prayed, "O Lord, open his eyes and let him see!" The Lord opened the young man's eyes, and when he looked up, he saw that the hillside around Elisha was filled with horses and chariots of fire. 2 Kings 6:17 nlt

What does that mean?

Elisha had great faith. He knew that God gives us things others cannot see. That gave Elisha courage, peace, and prayer power.

So, what?

Don't worry about anything. God has you in His hands. He is doing things you may not see. Just believe.

1-2 Chronicles

Who wrote 1-2 Chronicles?

The books don't say—but most people believe it was Ezra the priest.

When were 1-2 Chronicles written?

The stories take place from about 2,500 to 3,000 years ago. The books were written about 2,500 years ago.

What are 1-2 Chronicles about?

One word: Israel.

In more words: These books tell the story of God's people from the very beginning—starting with Adam. Then they turn to Israel's greatest king—David, from the tribe of Judah. Here we learn of God's promise: Kings from David's family will rule forever and ever.

When David's son Solomon becomes king, he builds a temple for God. But after Solomon dies, the nation splits. Many kings (and one queen) lead the two countries, called Israel and Judah. Sadly, most of the leaders are very bad, and foreign countries take over both Israel and Judah. After many years, the Persian king Cyrus lets the Jews go back to rebuild their destroyed temple.

1–2 Chronicles also tells us about

- King Saul's death in a battle
- God's glory filling the temple
- a godly leader named Josiah, who became king at age eight

What's an important verse from 1-2 Chronicles?

"I will put him over My house and in My nation forever. And his throne will last forever."
1 CHRONICLES 17:14 NLV

What does that mean?

David was from Israel's "tribe [or family] of Judah." He was a great king and very special to God. So God promised David that people from the king's family—Judah—would always rule. This promise came true! Jesus—a descendant of David—will rule forever and ever!

So, what?

You can always trust God. When He makes a promise, He keeps it!

Ezra

Who wrote Ezra?

The book doesn't say—but some people believe it was Ezra, a priest.

When was Ezra written?

About 2,500 years ago.

What's Ezra about?

One word: Redoing.

In more words: About 50 years earlier, Babylonians had destroyed Jerusalem. They took the Jews away from their homes. But now Persia's King Cyrus is the most powerful. He lets 42,000 Jews go back to Israel to redo the temple. About 70 years later, Ezra and 2,000 more Jews go back home. There the priest teaches God's law to His people.

Ezra also tells us about

- Jews getting their temple treasures back
- enemies bullying the Israelites
- the temple being rebuilt in Jerusalem
- people shaking after hearing God's Word

What's an important verse from Ezra?

I was ashamed to ask King Artaxerxes for soldiers and horsemen. They could have kept us safe from enemies on the road. But we had told the king that our God would keep us safe. We had said, "The gracious hand of our God helps everyone who looks to him." EZRA 8:22

What does that mean?

God gives us work to do. When we walk out in faith, God gives us all we need to do the job.

So, what?

Put your faith to work. Pray to God with all your heart. He will help you do whatever you need to do—or redo!

Nehemiah

Who wrote Nehemiah?

The words are Nehemiah's. But some say they were put down on paper by Ezra the priest.

When was Nehemiah written?

About 2,500 years ago.

What's Nehemiah about?

One word: Walls.

In more words: Nehemiah is the Persian king's wine taster. Knowing Jerusalem's walls are broken, Nehemiah is very sad. So King Artaxerxes lets him go home to rebuild the walls. The Israelites' enemies try many things to stop the work. But God is with His people. So the walls are built in 52 days. And all God's people rejoice!

Nehemiah also tells us about

- how the gates of Jerusalem had been burned with fire
- armored men with spears, bows, and swords guarding the workers
- enemies plotting to kill Nehemiah
- Nehemiah warning the people against forgetting God's laws

What's an important verse from Nehemiah?

"The God of heaven will give us success. We serve him. So we'll start rebuilding the walls." NEHEMIAH 2:20

What does that mean?

Nehemiah knew deep in his heart that God would make sure the walls would be rebuilt. When we are sure God will do something, it gives us confidence. And with confidence in God and ourselves, we can do anything!

So, what?

If you are sure God wants you to succeed, you will! Nothing can stand in your way!

Esther

Who wrote Esther?

The book doesn't say—but some people believe it may have been Ezra or Nehemiah.

When was Esther written?

About 2,500 years ago.

What's Esther about?

One word: Courage.

In more words: Esther was a beautiful Jewish orphan with one relative—cousin Mordecai. Persia's King Xerxes picked Esther to be his queen. He didn't know she was Jewish. When the king's official Haman tried to have all the Jews killed, Esther was very brave. She asked the king to save her—and her people. And he did!

Esther also tells us about
- a woman's life in the king's palace
- how Mordecai saved King Xerxes
- Haman being hanged for his evil deeds
- Jews celebrating with the first feast of Purim

What's an important verse from Esther?

"If you keep quiet at this time, help will come to the Jews from another place. But you and your father's house will be destroyed. Who knows if you have not become queen for such a time as this?" ESTHER 4:14 NLV

What does that mean?

Esther could either be brave and speak to the king or keep quiet and lose her life. She trusted God. So she stepped out in faith and did the right thing. So God blessed her—and her people!

So, what?

When you are in a hard place, it may be because God wants to use you. So be courageous and do good—and blessings will follow!

Who wrote Job?

The book doesn't say.

When was Job written?

No one really knows. But many believe it's one of the
oldest books in the Bible—maybe over 4,000 years old.

What's Job about?

One word: Suffering.

In more words: Job is a rich man with ten children and lots of animals. And he is a very good man—so good that God points him out to Satan. The devil asks God to let him test Job's faith. God agrees. So Satan wipes out all of Job's animals and children. Then Satan attacks Job's health. But no matter what, Job keeps his faith in God.

Job also tells us about

- Job's wife, who tells Job to "curse God and die"
- Job's friends, who try to blame Job for his own problems
- God coming to Job in a whirlwind
- God blessing Job with more than ever before!

What's an important verse from Job?

"Even though He would kill me, yet I will trust in Him."
JOB 13:15 NLV

What does that mean?

No matter how much Job suffered, he kept trusting God. So God rewarded Job's faith and hope. God gave Job ten more children and two times the animals he'd had before.

So, what?

Even if you are being good, bad things may happen. But if you keep trusting God, He will reward your faith!

Psalms

Who wrote Psalms?

More than one person. Almost half are "of David." Other authors are Solomon, Moses, Asaph, Ethan, and the sons of Korah. Many psalms don't say anything about who wrote them.

When was Psalms written?

About 2,500 to 3,400 years ago.

What's Psalms about?

One word: Praise!

In more words: God inspired lots of different people to write these 150 poems! At least 73 of them were written by, for, or about David—Israel's greatest king. Some psalms talk of joy. Some talk of sadness. But almost all are written from the heart and end on a note of praise.

Psalms also tells us about

- how God is a shepherd of His people
- the power of God and His Word
- angels coming to our rescue
- how much humans need God

What's an important verse from Psalms?

Your word is like a lamp that shows me the way. It is like a light that guides me. PSALM 119:105

What does that mean?

Sometimes we don't know which way to turn. It may be because we are sad, angry, lonely, or afraid. Fortunately, there is a psalm for each feeling we have. When we read the psalms, we not only feel better but find God lighting our way. And that leads to praise!

So, what?

When you need help, go to God through the psalms. With His light, you will find your way and burst out in praise.

Proverbs

Who wrote Proverbs?

Most of these proverbs were written by Solomon. Others were written by Agur, King Lemuel, and other wise people.

When was Proverbs written?

King Solomon wrote his about 3,000 years ago. King Hezekiah's staff copied down the remaining proverbs about 200 years later.

What's Proverbs about?

One word: Wisdom.

In more words: Proverbs tells us how to live our lives in a way that pleases God. The main writer of the book, King Solomon, was the wisest man ever! Proverbs tell us how to treat other people, work hard, rest often, and bring up children. Any problem we may have is covered in these pages.

Proverbs also tells us about
- how to find wisdom
- what happens to fools
- what a true friend is
- how wonderful a good wife can be

What's an important verse from Proverbs?

Trust in the LORD with all your heart; do not depend on your own understanding. Seek his will in all you do, and he will show you which path to take. PROVERBS 3:5–6 NLT

What does that mean?

To be truly wise, we must totally trust God. If we go to Him for all of the answers, He will lead us on the right path every time!

So, what?

If you aren't sure what to do, ask God. He'll tell you what to do—and it will always be the right thing! Now that's wisdom!

Ecclesiastes

Who wrote Ecclesiastes?

The book says it was written by David's son and the wisest king of Israel in Jerusalem. So most people believe it was Solomon.

When was Ecclesiastes written?

About 3,000 years ago.

What's Ecclesiastes about?

One word: Emptiness.

In more words: A human being's life without God is totally empty. We could have all the riches in the world—everything we ever wanted. But without God, we have nothing and are nothing. Solomon says we will only have a full life if we obey God and put Him first in everything.

Ecclesiastes also tells us about

- everything having a beginning and an end
- nothing making sense without God
- how only God can make us totally happy
- godly wisdom being an awesome thing

What's an important verse from Ecclesiastes?

And here's the final thing I want to say. Have respect for God and obey his commandments. That's what everyone should do. ECCLESIASTES 12:13

What does that mean?

When we respect God and do what He tells us, we will have nothing to fear. That's because we're doing what He wants us to do. Then we will have a full life and be full of joy. And that will please God—now and forever.

So, what?

Everyone is born with a God-shaped hole in their heart. Put God there and you will never be empty or alone.

Song of Solomon

Who wrote Song of Solomon?

The book doesn't say—but most people believe it was Solomon. Others believe this book may just have been for or about him.

When was Song of Solomon written?

About 3,000 years ago.

What's Song of Solomon about?

One word: Love.

In more words: King Solomon is going to marry a young, beautiful woman. They love each other very much. The eight chapters of this poem tell us about their romance and wedding. It speaks of all their joy, sadness, and excitement. The love they share is very powerful.

Song of Solomon also tells us about

- the bride, from a place called Shulam
- the groom named Solomon
- their wedding day
- the happy couple's journey to Jerusalem

What's an important verse from Song of Solomon?

Love is like a blazing fire. It burns like a mighty flame. No amount of water can put it out.

Song of Solomon 8:6–7

What does that mean?

True love cannot be destroyed. It cannot be bought. It will never let us go. The love Solomon and his bride shared gives us a picture of how much God loves us. The joy they share in each other is the joy we can find and share in God.

So, what?

God loves you so much He sent Jesus to save you. Give your heart to Him and share in His joy!

Isaiah

Who wrote Isaiah?

A prophet named Isaiah.

When was Isaiah written?

About 2,700 years ago.

What's Isaiah about?

One word: Messiah.

In more words: Isaiah was a prophet of God. God would give him a message. Then Isaiah would tell the Israelites what God had said. The bad news was that God would punish people for the bad things they did. The good news was that a Messiah would save them. And the Messiah that Isaiah describes sounds just like Jesus!

Isaiah also tells us about

- his vision of God's awesome throne in heaven
- angels called seraphim—they each had six wings!
- a virgin giving birth
- how someday there will be peace—when wolves will hang out with lambs

What's an important verse from Isaiah?

The Spirit of the LORD and King is on me. The LORD has anointed me to tell the good news to poor people.
ISAIAH 61:1

What does that mean?

Isaiah was telling the Israelites that someday a Messiah would come and preach good news to them. About 700 years after Isaiah told them this, Jesus came into our world. He preached to the Jews from Isaiah 61. Then He told the Jews that Isaiah's prophecy (what a prophet says will happen in the future) had just been fulfilled.

So, what?

Want good news? Open your Bible. There you'll find Jesus—God's Word. He's the Messiah sent to love and lift you up!

Jeremiah

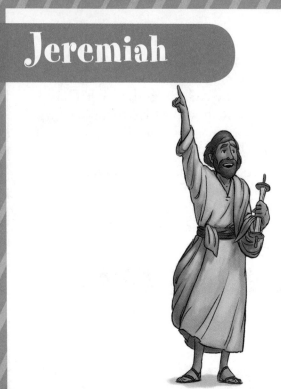

Who wrote Jeremiah?

Jeremiah, a prophet, wrote this book with the help of Baruch, a kind of secretary.

When was Jeremiah written?

About 2,600 years ago.

What's Jeremiah about?

One word: Plans.

In more words: Jeremiah was a prophet. He told the people of Judah what would happen in their future. Because of the evil the people of Judah had done, their enemy would take them as prisoners. In the end, Babylonians invade Judah, capture all the people, and take them away from their homes.

Jeremiah also tells us about
- King Jehoiakim cutting up, then burning, Jeremiah's book
- God telling Jeremiah to write the book again
- Jeremiah being kept prisoner in a muddy well
- Jeremiah escaping to Egypt

What's an important verse from Jeremiah?

"For I know the plans I have for you," says the Lord, "plans for well-being and not for trouble, to give you a future and a hope." JEREMIAH 29:11 NLV

What does that mean?

No matter what happened to the Jews, God wanted them to know He would not forget them. He had good plans for them. God sending Jesus to save His people was a part of those plans. Our God is a god of hope and love. He will never stop trying to bring us back to Him.

So, what?

God loves you and knows what's best for you. That's why He wants you to obey Him. He has good plans—just for you!

Lamentations

Who wrote Lamentations?

The book doesn't say—but most people believe it was Jeremiah.

When was Lamentations written?

About 2,600 years ago.

What's Lamentations about?

One word: Sadness.

In more words: Jeremiah had told the people of Judah what would happen if they kept disobeying God. And what the prophet had said came true: The nation of Judah was destroyed and its people taken away. Jeremiah saw it with his own eyes. It made him cry. That's why Jeremiah is called "the weeping prophet."

Lamentations also tells us about
- the people of Jerusalem becoming slaves
- the ruin of the temple of God
- people lying in piles of ash
- how the people who once danced were now very sad

What's an important verse from Lamentations?

The LORD loves us very much. So we haven't been completely destroyed. His loving concern never fails. LAMENTATIONS 3:22

What does that mean?

When Jeremiah was focused on himself and the trouble all around him, he got very sad. But then he thought about God. Once Jeremiah looked up to God, he remembered all the good God had done for him and the people of Judah. Somehow God still loved them! Jeremiah knew God would never leave them.

So, what?

If you ever feel sad, look up. Remember how much God loves you! He will always be with you! That's something to be happy about!

Ezekiel

Who wrote Ezekiel?

The book says it was written by the priest Ezekiel.

When was Ezekiel written?

About 2,600 years ago.

What's Ezekiel about?

One word: Newness.

In more words: Ezekiel was a priest and a prophet. He had been taken prisoner and sent to Babylon. He had many visions. He told the Israelites that Jerusalem would be destroyed. When it was, Ezekiel told the people that better days were ahead. They would have a wonderful future with God and His glory. They would have a new start.

Ezekiel also tells us about

- a vision of creatures, each with four faces and four wings
- how the people's sins had led them to lose their homeland
- God telling Ezekiel to eat a book
- dry bones rising up to form a great army!

What's an important verse from Ezekiel?

"I will give you new hearts. I will give you a new spirit that is faithful to me. I will remove your stubborn hearts from you. I will give you hearts that obey me." EZEKIEL 36:26

What does that mean?

God wants us to have completely new hearts—and new spirits. Ones that will be true to Him. Ones that will obey Him. That's why God sent Jesus—to totally change us!

So, what?

When you find yourself being stubborn with God, stop. Have a change of heart. Obey Him. He will love the new you!

Daniel

Who wrote Daniel?

The book doesn't say—but most people believe it was Daniel.

When was Daniel written?

About 2,600 years ago.

What's Daniel about?

One word: Power.

In more words: Daniel was a young man sent to Babylon. Three of his friends—Shadrach, Meshach, and Abednego—went with him. Daniel was very brave. God gave him much wisdom and many visions. He could even tell people what their dreams meant. Daniel served three kings—Nebuchadnezzar, Belshazzar, and Cyrus.

Daniel also tells us about

- God saving Shadrach, Meshach, and Abednego from a fiery furnace
- fingers writing a message for the king on a wall
- angels shutting the mouths of lions
- Daniel's vision of four beasts

What's an important verse from Daniel?

"If we are thrown into the blazing furnace, the God whom we serve is able to save us. He will rescue us from your power, Your Majesty." DANIEL 3:17 NLT

What does that mean?

King Nebuchadnezzar wanted Shadrach, Meshach, and Abednego to worship a statue. When they wouldn't, the king threw them into a furnace. But a fourth person in the fire—like the Son of God—kept them safe! When we dare to follow God, His power saves and strengthens us.

So, what?

With God, you can be brave. Dare to follow Him! When you stick close to Him, His power will protect you.

Hosea

Who wrote Hosea?

The book doesn't say—but most people believe it was Hosea.

When was Hosea written?

About 2,700 years ago.

What's Hosea about?

One word: Loyalty.

In more words: Hosea was a prophet of God. He lived in the northern nation of Israel. He married a woman, Gomer, who was not loyal to him. She was like the people of Israel who were not loyal to their God. They worshipped idols instead of God. So God told the people, through Hosea, that they would be punished. But if they would call on God, He'd answer.

Hosea also tells us about
- the birth of Hosea's children
- the wickedness of Israel
- the punishment of God's people
- Israel's future—full of blessings

What's an important verse from Hosea?

"My people always wander away from me. But I will put an end to that. My anger has turned away from them. Now I will love them freely." HOSEA 14:4

What does that mean?

The Israelites had turned away from God. That made God angry. But Hosea said if they returned to God, He would forgive them. And He would bless them! God is loyal to us even when we aren't loyal to Him.

So, what?

Are you loyal to God? Or do you worship something other than Him? If you have wandered away from Him, stop. Turn back. He'll give you another chance. And He'll bless you for your loyalty!

Joel

Who wrote Joel?

The book says it was written by the prophet Joel.

When was Joel written?

No one knows for sure. Many people believe it may have been written about 2,600 years ago.

What's Joel about?

One word: Repentance.

In more words: *Repent* means to turn away from doing bad things. Joel was telling the people of Judah that unless they repented, God would punish them. Israel would be punished, too. Afterward God would give back everything they had lost.

Joel also tells us about

- a swarm of locusts eating all the farmers' crops
- a darkness that would spread across the land
- lack of water all over the land
- God blessing the people once again

What's an important verse from Joel?

Return to the LORD your God, for he is merciful and compassionate, slow to get angry and filled with unfailing love. He is eager to relent and not punish. . . . The LORD says, "I will give you back what you lost." JOEL 2:13, 25 NLT

What does that mean?

Sometimes God allows bad things to happen so that we will repent and come back to Him. If we do, He will forgive us and make up for what we have lost. That's what He promised His people then—and still promises us today.

So, what?

Is there something you need to repent of? If so, do it! Then watch how God blesses you!

Amos

Who wrote Amos?

The book says it was written by a shepherd named Amos.

When was Amos written?

About 2,800 years ago.

What's Amos about?

One word: Fairness.

In more words: Amos is a prophet who tells off Israel's rich and powerful. God doesn't like their behavior. The rich and powerful are worshipping idols. They are also bullying God's prophets and not being fair to the poor. Because of their bad behavior, trouble is coming to them.

What's an important verse from Amos?

Do what is good and run from evil so that you may live! AMOS 5:14 NLT

What does that mean?

Part of doing good is being fair to other people. True followers of God and Jesus obey the Golden Rule. They treat others as they themselves want to be treated.

So, what?

When you do good and help others, God will help you.

Obadiah

Who wrote Obadiah?

The book says it was written by Obadiah. Obadiah means "servant of God."

When was Obadiah written?

Some think it was written about 2,600 years ago.

What's Obadiah about?

One word: Payback.

In more words: The people who lived in Edom were offspring of Esau. He was the twin brother of Jacob. Those boys never got along with each other—and neither did their children's children. When Babylon raided Jerusalem, Edom helped.

What's an important verse from Obadiah?

"You will be paid back for what you have done."
Obadiah 15

What does that mean?

God was very faithful to His people. He had told them long ago that He would bless those that blessed Israel and curse those that cursed Israel.

So, what?

You can rely on God. He always keeps His promises.

Jonah

Who wrote Jonah?

The book doesn't say. It's Jonah's story, but people aren't sure if he's the person who wrote it.

When was Jonah written?

About 2,800 years ago.

What's Jonah about?

One word: Mercy.

In more words: God tells Jonah to go to Nineveh. He wants him to tell the people there that if they don't behave, God will destroy them. But Jonah runs in the other direction. Later he gets to Nineveh, gives the people God's message, and they repent (turn back from their evil ways). So God, in His mercy (kindness), spares the city.

Jonah also tells us about
- sailors throwing Jonah into the sea during a storm
- a giant fish swallowing Jonah
- Jonah's decision to obey God
- God telling the fish to spit Jonah up on dry land

What's an important verse from Jonah?

"You are a kind and loving God Who shows pity. I knew that You are slow to anger and are filled with loving-kindness, always ready to change Your mind and not punish." JONAH 4:2 NLV

What does that mean?

The people of Nineveh repented. So Jonah's prophecy did not come true. God loves us so much that He is always willing to give people second chances. He even gave Jonah another chance!

So, what?

Remember that God loves you. He is full of mercy. He will always give you another chance!

Micah

Who wrote Micah?

The book doesn't say—but some people believe it was the prophet Micah. Others say Micah asked someone to write it down for him.

When was Micah written?

About 2,700 years ago.

What's Micah about?

One word: Deliverance.

In more words: Israel and Judah are worshipping idols and cheating the poor. This does not make God happy—at all! So Micah tells them they will be destroyed. But God will save some of the Israelites. And He will give them a good king to rule over them.

Micah also tells us about

- God destroying carved idols worshipped by His people
- God's people being taken prisoner
- people flowing to the Lord's mountain home
- what God wants—His people to be fair, kind, and walking with Him

What's an important verse from Micah?

"Bethlehem Ephrathah, you are too little to be among the family groups of Judah. But from you One will come who will rule for Me in Israel. His coming was planned long ago, from the beginning." MICAH 5:2 NLV

What does that mean?

Seven hundred years before Jesus was born, Micah named His birthplace. Jesus coming to save people was God's plan from the beginning of time. No matter how we behave, God is always out to deliver us!

So, what?

With Jesus, you need not worry about anything. He's part of God's plan to save you—and everyone else who believes!

Nahum

Who wrote Nahum?

The book says it's a "vision" God gave Nahum.

When was Nahum written?

About 2,600 years ago.

What's Nahum about?

One word: Choice.

In more words: This book is a sort of follow-up to Jonah's. The city in trouble is Nineveh. When Jonah went there, he told the people that unless they changed their ways, God would destroy their city. So they chose to stop sinning. But many years later, they were misbehaving again. To be against God brings trouble. To be with Him brings blessing.

What's an important verse from Nahum?

The Lord is good, a safe place in times of trouble. And He knows those who come to Him to be safe. NAHUM 1:7 NLV

What does that mean?

God knows who is on His side. For those people, He is a place where they can run and be safe.

So, what?

Choose to follow God. You will be blessed.

Habakkuk

Who wrote Habakkuk?

A prophet named Habakkuk.

When was Habakkuk written?

About 2,600 years ago.

What's Habakkuk about?

One word: Trust.

In more words: The people of Judah have been evil. So God has a plan: He's going to use the even more evil Babylonians to punish Judah. The prophet Habakkuk does not understand God's plan. Then it hits him! He doesn't have to understand everything God does. Habakkuk just has to trust the Lord. God always works things out for good.

What's an important verse from Habakkuk?

"But the righteous will live by their faithfulness to God." HABAKKUK 2:4 NLT

What does that mean?

Sometimes we ask God, "Why?" But no matter how bad things seem, we can trust that God is in control.

So, what?

Don't worry about anything. Everything—including you— is in God's huge hands! He won't let you down.

Zephaniah

Who wrote Zephaniah?

The books says a prophet named Zephaniah wrote it. He might have been the great-great-grandson of good King Hezekiah.

When was Zephaniah written?

About 2,600 years ago.

What's Zephaniah about?

One word: Hypocrites.

In more words: Once in a while, the people of Judah would behave. Later they went back to their evil ways. This was because their change for the good was never deep. It did not reach their hearts. They were hypocrites—people who pretend to be what they are not. So Zephaniah told the people God would punish them.

Zephaniah also tells us about
- the coming "day of the Lord"
- all the nations that would be destroyed
- how true seekers of God might be spared
- God being in our midst

What's an important verse from Zephaniah?

"For the LORD your God is living among you. He is a mighty savior. He will take delight in you with gladness. With his love, he will calm all your fears. He will rejoice over you with joyful songs." ZEPHANIAH 3:17 NLT

What does that mean?

God knows what is really in people's hearts. He is with those who are true believers. Because of His love, they have nothing to fear! They make Him so happy He can't help but sing!

So, what?

Go deep with God. Stick to Him no matter what is going on around you. Then open your ears. Listen for His song!

Haggai

Who wrote Haggai?

The book says the prophet Haggai wrote it.

When was Haggai written?

About 2,500 years ago.

What's Haggai about?

One word: Perseverance.

In more words: *Perseverance* means to keep doing something until you succeed. And that's what Haggai told the Jews to do. When they came back to their homeland, they needed to keep rebuilding God's temple until it was finished! While they were working, God would be with them. And when they were finished, He would bless them!

Haggai also tells us about

- people who built their homes before working on God's
- a drought in the land
- the Lord giving people courage
- Zerubbabel, the governor of Judah

What's an important verse from Haggai?

"Be strong, all you people still left in the land. And now get to work, for I am with you, says the LORD of Heaven's Armies." HAGGAI 2:4 NLT

What does that mean?

God saw that the people were selfish. They cared more about themselves than Him. So the Lord told Haggai to talk to the people of Judah. The prophet let them know God wanted them to work on His home. He would give them the strength to do it. When they finished, He would give them rain. Then they would have crops and food.

So, what?

God wants you to put Him first in your life. When you do, He will bless you.

Zechariah

Who wrote Zechariah?

The book says a prophet and priest named Zechariah wrote it. Some people believe another person wrote chapters 9–14.

When was Zechariah written?

About 2,500 years ago.

What's Zechariah about?

One word: Arrival.

In more words: Zechariah told the Jews returning home to rebuild God's house. He also had eight visions. He told the Jews things about the Messiah who would arrive someday. When Jesus arrived, people saw many of Zechariah's predictions come true!

Zechariah also tells us about

- a flying scroll
- the Messiah riding a donkey into Jerusalem
- the Savior being hung on a cross
- Roman soldiers poking the Messiah with a spear

What's an important verse from Zechariah?

"I will save you. You will be a blessing to others. Do not be afraid. Let your hands be strong so that you can do my work." ZECHARIAH 8:13

What does that mean?

God reminded His people that He would take care of them. He gave them courage to work on rebuilding His temple. He would make them strong so that they could finish the job. God also told them that one day the Messiah's glory would fill that temple.

So, what?

Whenever you feel weak, go to God. He will give you the strength—and courage—to do what He has called you to do.

Malachi

Who wrote Malachi?

The book says it was written by the prophet Malachi.

When was Malachi written?

About 2,450 years ago.

What's Malachi about?

One word: Reform.

In more words: To *reform* means to change for the better. And that's what God wanted His people to be— better. God's priests were misbehaving. And the people were following their example. So God told Malachi to give them a message: Stop misbehaving, return to God, and get ready to meet your Messiah.

Malachi also tells us about
- how much God loves His people
- the Lord never changing
- people being blessed as they give to God
- a book of remembrance

What's an important verse from Malachi?

"You have turned away from my rules. You have not obeyed them. You have lived that way ever since the days of your people long ago. Return to me. Then I will return to you," says the LORD who rules over all. MALACHI 3:7

What does that mean?

God is not happy when His people disobey Him. He wants us to return to Him with all of our heart, strength, mind, and soul. When we do, we find Him right there with us!

So, what?

Run to God right now! Ask Him what needs to be changed. Give Him all that you have and are. When you do, you'll find Him closer than ever before.

Matthew

Who wrote Matthew?

The book doesn't say—but most people believe it was
Matthew, a tax collector. Matthew is also known by the
name Levi.

When was Matthew written?

About 1,940 years ago.

What's Matthew about?

One word: Fulfillment.

In more words: Old Testament prophets told what the coming Messiah would be like and what He would do. Matthew tells the Jews how Jesus fulfilled (lived up to) all those prophecies. This book is the first of four *Gospels* (a word meaning "good news"). It begins by showing how Jesus is related to King David and Abraham.

Matthew also tells us about

- the wise men who visited baby Jesus
- Jesus' Sermon on the Mount
- Jesus dying on the cross
- an angel rolling back the stone door on Jesus' tomb

What's an important verse from Matthew?

"Keep on asking, and you will receive what you ask for. Keep on seeking, and you will find. Keep on knocking, and the door will be opened to you." MATTHEW 7:7 NLT

What does that mean?

God loves us very much. When we keep on asking Him for things, we will get what He wants for us. When we keep our eyes on Him, we will find what we are looking for.

So, what?

Jesus is your King. More powerful than an angel, He can open any door for you. But He wants you to want Him more than anything else.

Mark

Who wrote Mark?

The book doesn't say—but most people believe it was John Mark, a missionary who traveled with Paul and Barnabas. He also worked with the apostle Peter.

When was Mark written?

About 1,950 years ago.

What's Mark about?

One word: Servant.

In more words: Mark's book was probably the first of the Gospels written. And it's the shortest one! Mark is writing to Gentiles (people who are not Jews), telling them that Jesus came to serve—not to be served. He served by healing people, driving out demons, and showing His power over nature.

Mark also tells us about

- Jesus choosing His 12 disciples (followers)
- the family of Jesus, who thought He was crazy
- Jesus calming a storm
- the women who visited Jesus' tomb

What's an important verse from Mark?

"Anyone who wants to be first must be the slave of everyone. Even the Son of Man did not come to be served. Instead, he came to serve others." MARK 10:44–45

What does that mean?

Jesus turned the world upside down. Before He came, people had thought it important to be important. But Jesus told them the most important thing was to serve others with love—not to have others serve us.

So, what?

To be a true follower of Jesus, you must serve others gladly. Who can you love and serve today?

Luke

Who wrote Luke?

The book doesn't say—but most people believe it was a non-Jewish doctor named Luke. He was a missionary and a friend of Paul the apostle.

When was Luke written?

About 1,940 years ago.

What's Luke about?

One word: Reporting.

In more words: Luke was a doctor who wanted Theophilus to know the facts of Jesus' story. So Luke's book is a true report of Jesus' life. Luke includes more of Jesus' parables (stories with a lesson) than any other Gospel writer. He even describes several miracles that the other Gospels don't mention.

Luke also tells us about

- the early years of John the Baptist
- lots of details about Jesus' birth
- Jesus as a boy
- the parables of the Good Samaritan and the Prodigal Son

What's an important verse from Luke?

"Master," Simon replied, "we worked hard all last night and didn't catch a thing. But if you say so, I'll let the nets down again." And this time their nets were so full of fish they began to tear! LUKE 5:5–6 NLT

What does that mean?

When we obey God, we find blessings—for us and for others. He knows what we're trying to do. So listen for His voice, follow His directions, and watch His goodness flow.

So, what?

Don't just listen to God. Obey Him in all that you do! Before you know it, you'll find blessings all around! That's a fact!

John

Who wrote John?

The book doesn't say—but most people believe it was the disciple John, the brother of James.

When was John written?

About 1,920 years ago.

What's John about?

One word: Christ.

In more words: John wrote this book so that people would believe Jesus was the Christ—God in human form. He writes that Jesus is the Word and that He made the universe. John was very close to Jesus. When Jesus was on the cross, He asked John to take care of His mother Mary.

John also tells us about

- Jesus turning water into wine at a wedding
- the story of the Samaritan woman at a well
- Lazarus being raised from the dead
- Jesus walking on the water during a storm

What's an important verse from John?

"God so loved the world that He gave His only Son. Whoever puts his trust in God's Son will not be lost but will have life that lasts forever." JOHN 3:16 NLV

What does that mean?

God loves each and every one of us. He loves us so much that He sent His only Son to save the world. People who trust in Jesus will live forever!

So, what?

God loves you so much. Just put your trust in Jesus. Accept Christ into your heart. Then you can live with Him forever and ever!

Acts

Who wrote Acts?

The book doesn't say—but most people believe it was a non-Jewish doctor named Luke. He was a missionary and a friend of Paul the apostle.

When was Acts written?

About 1,940 years ago, but covering earlier events.

One word: Church.

In more words: The book begins with Jesus floating up to heaven. Ten days later, the Holy Spirit comes down from heaven and fires up Jesus' followers. The disciples now have power and courage to preach about Jesus. That day, 3,000 people become followers of Jesus. And the Christian church is born!

Acts also tells us about

- Saul being blinded, then becoming the Christian named Paul
- Christians being persecuted (treated badly for believing in Jesus)
- Jesus' followers doing miracles
- Paul being shipwrecked on the island of Malta

What's an important verse from Acts?

"You will receive power when the Holy Spirit comes into your life." ACTS 1:8 NLV

What does that mean?

When people believe that Jesus is their Savior, the Holy Spirit comes into their lives. He powers them up. Then they have the courage to tell others of the peace and love of God!

So, what?

If you believe in Jesus, the Holy Spirit lives inside you. You have the power. You have the courage. You can do the things God wants you to do!

Romans

Who wrote Romans?

The book says it was written by the apostle Paul. His friend Tertius wrote down the letter for him.

When was Romans written?

About 1,950 years ago.

What's Romans about?

One word: Gospel.

In more words: Paul wrote this letter to believers in the city of Rome. He wanted to tell them God's Gospel ("good news")—that God sent Jesus to save all people. Those who believe in Jesus, even people who are not Jews, can now be right with God.

Romans also tells us about

- how Christ died for us while we were still enemies of God
- how we all need forgiveness—since we all make mistakes
- eternal life for all who belong to Christ
- the Holy Spirit understanding even our groans

What's an important verse from Romans?

Nothing at all can ever separate us from God's love because of what Christ Jesus our Lord has done.
ROMANS 8:39

What does that mean?

Nothing can keep us away from God's love. No angels or demons. Nothing today or tomorrow. No power at all or anything else in this world. God's love will always be with us. And that's the best news ever!

So, what?

There's nothing you have to do to earn God's love. He loved you yesterday. He loves you today. He will love you tomorrow. Nothing can stop His love! That's the Gospel truth!

1 Corinthians

Who wrote 1 Corinthians?

The book says it was written by the apostle Paul, with the help of a man named Sosthenes.

When was 1 Corinthians written?

About 1,960 years ago.

What's 1 Corinthians about?

One word: Behavior.

In more words: Paul had helped to begin a church in Corinth. This is Paul's first letter to the believers there. They were misbehaving. Some were arguing about who should be the church leader. Others were taking fellow believers to court.

1 Corinthians also tells us about
- believers having the mind of Christ
- not judging or bullying others
- God always giving us a way out from sin
- each believer having a spiritual gift

What's an important verse from 1 Corinthians?

The three most important things to have are faith, hope and love. But the greatest of them is love.
1 CORINTHIANS 13:13

What does that mean?

God is love. And His love is wonderful. So is the love we have for each other. It helps us to forgive others—and for them to forgive us. It helps us to be kind and patient. It never fails. It is the greatest thing ever! For God is love.

So, what?

God has filled you with His love. In fact, it is flowing over. So let it spill onto someone else today. Find someone to be kind to. Sharing God's love—now that's good behavior!

2 Corinthians

Who wrote 2 Corinthians?

The book says it was written by the apostle Paul, with Timothy's help.

When was 2 Corinthians written?

About 1,960 years ago.

What's 2 Corinthians about?

One word: Troublemakers.

In more words: This is Paul's second letter to the church at Corinth. Some troublemakers were saying bad things about Paul. They didn't think he should be in charge. So Paul tells them how Jesus called him to lead. Paul tells them how much he has suffered for Jesus.

2 Corinthians also tells us about

- each believer being a treasure in a clay jar
- Paul forgiving the troublemakers
- a man (probably Paul) being shown the highest heaven
- Paul being whipped, stoned, beaten, and shipwrecked

What's an important verse from 2 Corinthians?

He answered me, "I am all you need. I give you My loving-favor. My power works best in weak people." I am happy to be weak and have troubles so I can have Christ's power in me. 2 CORINTHIANS 12:9 NLV

What does that mean?

Eight times Paul asked God to take away trouble he had in his body. But God told Paul that He—God—was all he needed. When we are at our weakest, Christ's power works at its best!

So, what?

Feeling weak? That's okay. Just count on God. He'll give you Christ's power. Then you will win—and Jesus will get all the applause!

Galatians

Who wrote Galatians?

The book says it was written by the apostle Paul.

When was Galatians written?

About 1,960 years ago.

What's Galatians about?

One word: Freedom.

In more words: Some Christians in Galatia had turned away from their freedom in Christ. They began to go back to the rules the Jews had to obey. And they tried to make other Christians follow those same old rules. Paul tells them that no one can be right with God by trying to follow Jewish laws.

Galatians also tells us about

- Christ living in and through us
- freedom in Christ, meaning walking in His Spirit
- living by the Spirit so we will not follow the wants of our bodies
- the fact that we harvest what we have planted

What's an important verse from Galatians?

You have been called to live in freedom, my brothers and sisters. But don't use your freedom to satisfy your sinful nature. Instead, use your freedom to serve one another in love. GALATIANS 5:13 NLT

What does that mean?

Jesus Christ has made us free. We no longer have to follow the Jewish laws to be right with God. But we are not to use that freedom to do bad things—we are to love others and do good things for them.

So, what?

Jesus has given you a new rule: Follow God's Spirit. He will lead you down all the right paths.

Ephesians

Who wrote Ephesians?

The book says it was written by the apostle Paul.

When was Ephesians written?

About 1,950 years ago, near the end of Paul's life.

What's Ephesians about?

One word: Oneness.

In more words: Paul had started the church in Ephesus. Now he is writing to tell them how the church members should live in peace with one another. And that—together—all churches make up Christ's "body." There is one body, one Spirit, one hope, one Lord, one faith, one baptism, and one God who rules over all!

Ephesians also tells us about

- God bringing together Jews and non-Jews
- grace being a gift from God, something we cannot earn
- the way children should obey their parents and slaves obey their masters
- the different pieces that make up the armor of God

What's an important verse from Ephesians?

God is able to do much more than we ask or think through His power working in us. EPHESIANS 3:20 NLV

What does that mean?

The power God used to raise Jesus from the dead is the same power He has given to us. All we have to do is believe in Jesus Christ and follow where God leads! Then He will do more than we could ever ask—or imagine!

So, what?

Trust God to help you as you do what He tells you. He will give you the confidence you need. Then watch His awesome power go to work!

Philippians

Who wrote Philippians?

The book says it was written by the apostle Paul and Timothy.

When was Philippians written?

About 1,950 years ago.

What's Philippians about?

One word: Joy.

In more words: Paul thanked the Philippians (people from a city called Philippi) for some money they had sent him. Then he told them to be full of joy no matter what happened. Paul wrote this letter from a prison in Rome. Even there, he found a way to rejoice. His secret? Focusing on Christ instead of his situation!

Philippians also tells us about
- Paul preaching boldly while in prison
- everyone someday bowing to Christ
- thinking only of things that are good
- how we can do anything through Christ who strengthens us

What's an important verse from Philippians?

Brothers and sisters, I don't consider that I have taken hold of it yet. But here is the one thing I do. I forget what is behind me. I push hard toward what is ahead of me.
PHILIPPIANS 3:13

What does that mean?

When our eyes are on what happened yesterday, we lose power. We are not focused on what is right in front of us. So Paul tells us to forget the past. Then reach out to grab hold of today.

So, what?

Don't worry about what happened yesterday. Just focus on Christ. He is pure joy.

Colossians

Who wrote Colossians?

The book says it was written by the apostle Paul and Timothy.

When was Colossians written?

About 1,950 years ago.

What's Colossians about?

One word: Leaders.

In more words: The church in Colossae had some bad teachers. They were mixing lies in with the truth of Christ. So Paul told them Christ is the big Boss. He is in charge of everything and everyone. He is the Lord of life. He is the Master of heaven. He is above angels. He is the image of God.

Colossians also tells us about
- Christ holding everything together
- all the treasures found in Christ
- Christ being all that we need
- angels, which are not to be worshipped

What's an important verse from Colossians?

Keep looking for the good things of heaven. This is where Christ is seated on the right side of God. Keep your minds thinking about things in heaven. Do not think about things on the earth. COLOSSIANS 3:1–2 NLV

What does that mean?

Lots of thoughts fill our minds. Paul says we should think only of heavenly things—like love, goodness, friendship, hope, and more! These are the real treasures. Not gold, money, or other earthly things that will someday fade away.

So, what?

Did you know that you are what you think? So think only of good things. That will make you more like Christ! And that's a good think!

1 Thessalonians

Who wrote 1 Thessalonians?

The book says it was written by the apostle Paul, Silvanus (or Silas), and Timothy.

When was 1 Thessalonians written?

About 1,960 years ago.

What's 1 Thessalonians about?

One word: Returning.

In more words: Paul wanted to encourage the believers in a city called Thessalonica. To give them hope and comfort, Paul reminded them that someday Jesus will return. So it is important that they live good lives. Then when Christ returns, they will live with Him in His kingdom!

1 Thessalonians also tells us about
- Jesus coming down from heaven
- believers who are dead rising first
- believers who are alive meeting Christ in the clouds
- living a life covered with faith, hope, and love

What's an important verse from 1 Thessalonians?

Brothers and sisters, we urge you to warn those who are lazy. Encourage those who are timid. Take tender care of those who are weak. Be patient with everyone.
1 THESSALONIANS 5:14 NLT

What does that mean?

God wants believers to be good people. One way to do that is to be like Christ. That means working hard, helping people, and never giving up on anyone! Then when Christ comes back, He'll know we're ready to rise with Him.

So, what?

When you help others, it's as if Christ is working through you to touch them. So the next time you see someone who needs help, don't hesitate. Step right in! God will return your kindness!

2 Thessalonians

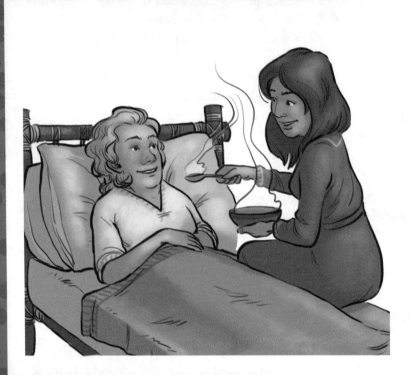

Who wrote 2 Thessalonians?

The book says it was written by the apostle Paul, Silvanus (or Silas), and Timothy.

When was 2 Thessalonians written?

About 1,960 years ago.

What's 2 Thessalonians about?

One word: Works.

In more words: After Paul's first letter to the Thessalonians, some believers there thought Jesus had already come back. So Paul told them He hasn't. But He will someday. Meanwhile, Paul told the believers to stay positive—to keep doing good and living right until Jesus returns.

2 Thessalonians also tells us about

- the troubles the believers were facing
- how proud Paul was of their great faith
- the appearance of the man of sin who will say He is God
- how God does and will keep us safe from the evil one

What's an important verse from 2 Thessalonians?

As for the rest of you, dear brothers and sisters, never get tired of doing good. 2 THESSALONIANS 3:13 NLT

What does that mean?

Sometimes, even when we are being and doing good, bad things happen. In good times and bad, God wants us to keep trusting Him. When we do, we will have peace. That's because we know He'll make everything turn out okay in the end.

So, what?

Trust God. He'll give you the energy and power to keep doing the right thing—in good times and bad.

1 Timothy

Who wrote 1 Timothy?

The book says it was written by the apostle Paul.

When was 1 Timothy written?

About 1,950 years ago.

What's 1 Timothy about?

One word: Pastors.

In more words: Timothy had worked with Paul many times. But now he was pastor of the church in Ephesus. So Paul wrote to Timothy, giving him some tips on running the church. He told him what kind of people could be leaders and how pastors should behave.

1 Timothy also tells us about

- how Paul used to hunt Christians
- Jesus using Paul as an example of God's great patience
- how we should pray for everyone, even kings
- taking care of widows and children

What's an important verse from 1 Timothy?

Love for money causes all kinds of evil. Some people want to get rich. They have wandered away from the faith. They have wounded themselves with many sorrows.
1 TIMOTHY 6:10

What does that mean?

Money is not evil. But the love of money is. When people are focused only on getting rich, unhappiness follows. They begin to count on money to always be there. But only God is always there for us. We can only have one master—God or money.

So, what?

For a happy life, stick close to God. He is your true source of joy. He is all you need.

2Timothy

Who wrote 2 Timothy?

The book says it was written by the apostle Paul.

When was 2 Timothy written?

About 1,950 years ago.

What's 2 Timothy about?

One word: Truth.

In more words: Paul is in prison in Rome. So he writes a letter to cheer up Timothy, who is like a son to him. Paul warns Timothy against false teachings and that trouble is coming. But God will stay with Timothy as long as Timothy stays close to God.

2 Timothy also tells us about

- God giving us a spirit of power, not of fear
- Paul's friends leaving him
- fighting the good fight of faith
- Paul wanting Timothy to visit him soon

What's an important verse from 2 Timothy?

God has breathed life into all of Scripture. It is useful for teaching us what is true. It is useful for correcting our mistakes. It is useful for making our lives whole again. It is useful for training us to do what is right. 2 TIMOTHY 3:16

What does that mean?

Scripture teaches us what is true and right. It trains us to be like Christ. If we study, use, and obey the words of the Bible, we will be prepared for anything!

So, what?

Read and study your Bible. Learn some verses by heart. Spinach is good for your muscles—but God's truth will make you even stronger!

Titus

Who wrote Titus?

The book says it was written by the apostle Paul.

When was Titus written?

About 1,950 years ago.

What's Titus about?

One word: Grace.

In more words: Young Titus was pastoring a church on the island of Crete, getting it in order. Paul tells Titus about grace—the love and kindness God gives us. Grace is a free gift from God, one we don't deserve. And there is nothing we can do to earn it.

Titus also tells us about

- what makes a good church leader
- people from Crete being evil, liars, and cheats
- older women teaching younger ones
- not looking down on someone because he or she is young

What's an important verse from Titus?

God gave the Holy Spirit to fill our lives through Jesus Christ, the One Who saves. Because of this, we are made right with God by His loving-favor. Now we can have life that lasts forever as He has promised. TITUS 3:6–7 NLV

What does that mean?

Because Jesus died on the cross, believers are cleansed from sin. Now nothing separates us from God—not even death! And the Holy Spirit can help us to live right. God's grace—what a wonderful gift!

So, what?

You are God's special child. He loves giving you good gifts—like grace! Ask the Spirit to help you live a special life.

Philemon

Who wrote Philemon?

The book says it was written by the apostle Paul.

When was Philemon written?

About 1,950 years ago.

What's Philemon about?

One word: Forgiving.

In more words: Paul is writing to a fellow believer named Philemon. Philemon's slave, Onesimus, had run away from him. Paul had met Onesimus when Paul was a prisoner in Rome. Now Paul is sending Onesimus back to his master. He writes hoping that Philemon will want to forgive his slave and welcome him with open arms.

Philemon also tells us about

- how much Onesimus helped Paul
- Onesimus being a new believer and like a brother to Paul
- Paul's willingness to repay anything Onesimus owed Philemon
- Mark and Luke being and working with Paul

What's an important verse from Philemon?

I did not want to keep him without word from you. I did not want you to be kind to me because you had to but because you wanted to. PHILEMON 14 NLV

What does that mean?

God doesn't want us doing good things because we have to. He wants us to do good things because we want to. When we want to do things God's way, it means our whole heart is in it. It means we have faith that His way is the right way.

So, what?

Living God's way gives us joy when we trust Him. Ask God whom He wants you to forgive today.

Hebrews

Who wrote Hebrews?

The book doesn't say who wrote it—but some believe it may have been either Paul, Luke, Barnabas, or Apollos.

When was Hebrews written?

About 1,945 years ago.

What's Hebrews about?

One word: Faith.

In more words: This letter was written to Jewish Christians. That's why it's called "Hebrews," which is another name for the Jews. The author tells readers how much better Jesus is than angels, Moses, and Jewish laws. Jesus is called the high priest of good things that are coming. One chapter has a long list of heroes of faith.

Hebrews also tells us about

- Enoch having walked with God
- Noah obeying God before seeing the floodwaters
- entertaining strangers because they might be angels
- Jesus Christ being the same yesterday, today, and tomorrow

What's an important verse from Hebrews?

Faith is being sure of what we hope for. It is being certain of what we do not see. HEBREWS 11:1

What does that mean?

Some people say, "Seeing is believing." But faith asks you to believe without seeing. We cannot see air or gravity, but we know they exist. God is the same way. We may not be able to see Him, but He is all around us. Amazing things happen when we have faith and hope in God—and His promises.

So, what?

Be sure of God and His promises. Then watch God work. You'll be amazed by your faith!

James

Who wrote James?

The book says it was written by James, who was probably Jesus' half brother.

When was James written?

About 1,950 years ago.

What's James about?

One word: Practice.

In more words: James wrote this letter to Jewish Christians. He tells them if their faith is true, good works will follow. He says Christians should practice their faith by watching what they say, making peace with everyone, praying, and helping the needy. Any problems should be seen as opportunities to grow in faith.

James also tells us about

- asking God for wisdom
- being doers of God's Word, not just hearers
- treating everyone equally
- standing up to the devil

What's an important verse from James?

Pray for one another so that you might be healed. The prayer of a godly person is powerful. It makes things happen. JAMES 5:16

What does that mean?

God wants us to help each other. That means praying for people who are sick or in trouble. When we are walking right with God, our prayers will have power and amazing things will happen.

So, what?

Do you know someone who is sick or has a problem? Practice your faith by praying for him or her. Don't worry about what to say. God knows your heart and the other person's need. There is no problem prayer cannot solve, no need it cannot meet. That's power!

1 Peter

Who wrote 1 Peter?

The book says it was written by the apostle Peter (Jesus' new name for Simon), with help from Silvanus.

When was 1 Peter written?

About 1,950 years ago.

What's 1 Peter about?

One word: Steadiness.

In more words: The Romans were giving Christians tons of trouble. So Peter tells believers to be steady in their faith. God is still in control. Trouble will only make a believer's faith stronger.

1 Peter also tells us about

- God protecting believers by His power
- believers respecting earthly leaders
- us following in Jesus' steps
- the devil prowling around like a lion

What's an important verse from 1 Peter?

So don't be proud. Put yourselves under God's mighty hand. Then he will honor you at the right time. Turn all your worries over to him. He cares about you.
1 PETER 5:6–7

What does that mean?

Sometimes we're not sure why certain things happen. But that's okay. We don't need to know why, because God does. So when troubles strikes, we just need to turn them over to God. Then, steady in our faith, we can stand firm against anything that comes our way.

So, what?

Got a problem? Don't hop around it. Take it to God; then stand steady on both feet. Know that He cares for you. Everything will be okay.

2 Peter

Who wrote 2 Peter?

The book says it was written by the apostle Peter, also known as Simon.

When was 2 Peter written?

About 1,945 years ago.

What's 2 Peter about?

One word: Twisting.

In more words: Peter was writing to warn believers. Some people were twisting the Good News of Jesus. Peter told believers to look to God's Word for the truth. Then they could avoid the false teachings. When Peter wrote this letter, he knew he would soon be killed.

2 Peter also tells us about

- Peter hearing God's voice from heaven
- fables that lead people away from God
- God knowing how to keep His people safe
- how God doesn't want anyone to be destroyed

What's an important verse from 2 Peter?

He gives us everything we need for life and for holy living. He gives it through His great power. As we come to know Him better, we learn that He called us to share His own shining-greatness and perfect life.

2 PETER 1:3 NLV

What does that mean?

The more we get to know God, the more we become like Christ. And the way to get to know God is to read His Word. His Word is truth. The Bible is our best teacher—and the right teacher!

So, what?

Spend time in God's Word. Then you'll shine like Christ! And that's the truth!

1 John

Who wrote 1 John?

The book doesn't say—but the church has long believed
the author was the apostle John.

When was 1 John written?

About 1,920 years ago.

What's 1 John about?

One word: Light.

In more words: John was writing to believers who had been listening to lies about the Good News. He reminded them that Jesus wasn't just a spirit. He had come to earth in the flesh. Many people had seen and touched Jesus. He was God in the form of man. And when we believe in and know Him, we are saved.

1 John also tells us about

- God forgiving our sins when we tell Him about them
- God's promise that believers will live forever
- believers being the children of God
- our prayers being a sure thing

What's an important verse from 1 John?

This is the message we heard from Jesus and now declare to you: God is light, and there is no darkness in him at all.
1 JOHN 1:5 NLT

What does that mean?

Light is pure, true, and right. And God is all of those things! Darkness is where things are hidden and where evil abides. With God in our lives, we need never be afraid. There is no darkness in Him.

So, what?

Remember that God chases away all darkness. Whenever you feel afraid, look for His light! Then shine with courage!

2 John

Who wrote 2 John?

The book doesn't say—but the church has long believed the author was the apostle John.

When was 2 John written?

About 1,920 years ago.

What's 2 John about?

One word: Commands.

In more words: This letter was written to a woman and her children. The writer is happy that these children are living by God's truth—the Bible. When we love God's Word, we are blessed.

What's an important verse from 2 John?

The way we show our love is to obey God's commands.
2 JOHN 6

What does that mean?

Jesus gave us two commands. First, to love God with all our heart, soul, and mind. Second, to love our neighbors as ourselves. If all of us would do that, this world would be a heavenly place!

So, what?

Tell God you love Him very, very much. Then be loving to everyone you meet.

3 John

Who wrote 3 John?

The book doesn't say—but the church has long believed the author was the apostle John.

When was 3 John written?

About 1,920 years ago.

What's 3 John about?

One word: Paths.

In more words: This letter was written to a friend named Gaius. John is very happy that Gaius and another man named Demetrius are being true to the faith. They have stayed on the right path. But John warns Gaius not to be like Diotrephes who is evil.

What's an important verse from 3 John?

Dear friend, don't be like those who do evil. Be like those who do good. 3 JOHN 11

What does that mean?

We tend to act like the people we hang around with. But no matter where we are or who we are with, God wants us to be good. And He wants us to be like His Son Jesus.

So, what?

Be a good example to your friends and brothers and sisters. Walk as Jesus walked.

Jude

Who wrote Jude?

The book says a man named Jude wrote it. He may have been Jesus' half brother.

When was Jude written?

About 1,930 years ago.

What's Jude about?

One word: Strength.

In more words: Jude is the brother of James. Jude is warning church members about people teaching lies. He called these false teachers complainers. They were behaving badly. They tried to get Christian believers to follow them. Jude wanted the true Christians to stay strong and not be fooled.

Jude also tells us about

- head angel Michael arguing with the devil over Moses' body
- people who think only of themselves
- how wrong desires can lead people into sin
- having kindness for those who doubt Jesus

What's an important verse from Jude?

Dear friends, build yourselves up in your most holy faith. Let the Holy Spirit guide and help you when you pray. JUDE 20

What does that mean?

By praying and praising God, we can become stronger in our faith. But sometimes we don't know how to pray. That's okay. The Holy Spirit can guide us. He'll help us to build up our spiritual muscles.

So, what?

When you are not sure what to pray, ask the Holy Spirit to help you. He understands everything you say—and everything you don't say! He'll give power to your prayers!

Revelation

Who wrote Revelation?

The book says it was written by a man named John, probably the apostle.

When was Revelation written?

About 1,920 years ago.

What's Revelation about?

One word: Visions.

In more words: Jesus Christ gave John a vision (or "revelation") of things that will happen one day. John writes down everything he sees. He begins the book with Jesus' message for seven churches. John ends the book by telling of a new heaven and a new earth.

Revelation also tells us about

- the Lamb in God's throne room
- a war in heaven
- a red dragon with seven heads and ten crowns
- two beasts, one from the sea, the other from the earth

What's an important verse from Revelation?

"God will take away all their tears. There will be no more death or sorrow or crying or pain. All the old things have passed away." REVELATION 21:4 NLV

What does that mean?

Someday God will do away with everything evil. Then there will be a new heaven and a new earth. God's home will be with all believers. There will be no more tears, death, or pain. Everything will be brand-new!

So, what?

If you are a believer, your name is in God's Book of Life. That means that someday you will live with God Himself on a brand-new earth. Now that's a home, a very sweet home. Can you imagine it?